Maui

Hiking, Waterfalls, Beaches

Follow Us @

Facebook, Twitter and Instagram

Introduction

This book was made purely out of love. It took us two years to hike, photograph and collect all the data. There is so much to do on our great island, and most of what you can enjoy is free. Best of all, everything in this book is **FREE** to do (except entry into Haleakala and Iao Park fees). There are not too many places you can travel to and have that luxury.

Every hike in the book, we did. We tried to grade each hike for the average person. If you are an avid hiker than some of these may be easy for you, if you don't hike at all there are hikes for you as well. We have yet to hike anywhere on Maui where the scenery has not been beautiful. There is so much to explore, this is just a taste of what the island has to offer.

Pictured are all the accessible beaches on the island that we are aware of. We have detailed and pictured 61 beaches, all unique in their own way. There are other beaches on the island, but they are either not easily accessed or they are hidden so that they are unknown to most, and most people would pass them by if they knew they were there at all.

We have traveled and explored the road to Hana many times. This is a gorgeous drive in its own, but if you pull over, park and get out of the car, there is so much more to see. We have included 37 waterfalls just on the road to Hana. We have listed them by mile markers without too much more detail. Most can be easily found by just getting out and looking. There are some that require short hikes, some a little slippery to get to and others, you need to google the name to find them.

We took every precaution to make sure that our directions were correct and that the descriptions fit the location. We are not perfect and apologize in advance if you find any mistakes while using this guide. We are sure that when you get done with your vacation, with this book in hand you will experience Maui in a way that will truly stay with you for years to come.

Table Of Contents

Waterfalls

Waterfalls Continued:

Beaches

GUIDE TO HIKES

Hiking Trails On Maui

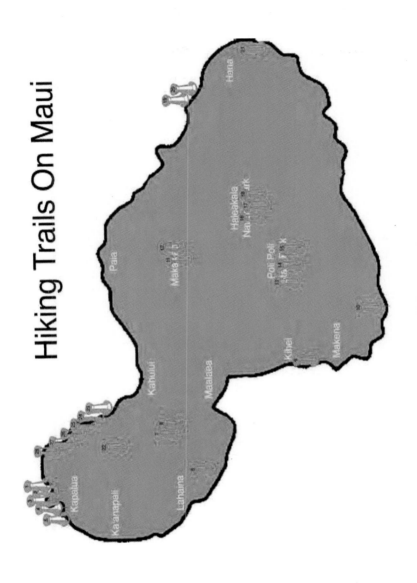

Maunalei Arboretum

Directions

Go North from Lahaina on
Honoapiilani Hwy. Turn
left on Office Rd. Then
turn Right on Village Rd
and the Kapalua Adventure
Center is on the right.

Distance: 0.5 miles
Elevation: 50ft
Trail: Easy

This is an easy trail and gorgeous views
from the lookout at the top of the trail.
This hike is on private property at
Kapalua and requires a free shuttle from
Kapalua Village Center. Reservations are
required because they only make 2 trips a
day to the trailhead and seating is limited.
This is a great thing because it makes the
hike private and protects the surroundings
and the trails by limited access.

The trail is well maintained, marked and
easy to follow. A narrow path, soft
ground to hike on and a very slight
elevation. There is a very detailed map at
the beginning of the trail and a bathroom
also. There are several markers that
identify the trees and foliage. Lots of
cover, narrow paths, very cool jungle like
path.

Honolua Ridge Trail

Distance:	2.5 miles
Elevation:	3504ft
Trail:	Easy

Directions

From Lahaina go North on Honoapiilani Highway. Turn left on Office Road then right on Village Road. The Kapalua Adventure Center is on the right.

This is an easy trail and gorgeous views from the lookout at the top of the trail. This hike is on private property at Kapalua and requires a free shuttle from Kapalua Village Center. Reservations are required because they only make 2 trips a day to the trailhead and seating is limited.

The trail is well maintained, marked and easy to follow, a narrow path, soft ground to hike on and a very slight elevation. There is a detailed map at the beginning of the trail and also a bathroom. There are several markers that identify the trees and foliage along this trail.

Mahana Ridge Trail

Distance:	6.5 miles round trip
Elevation:	2750ft
Trail:	Moderate to Difficult

Honoapiilani Hwy to Lahaina then drive North past Kaanapali & Kahana turn left at signs into Kapalua Resort which is Office Road. Turn right into Kapalua Adventure Center parking lot to catch shuttle.

This is a moderate to difficult only because of the distance. You can start this hike from the visitors center and hike up and back or take the free shuttle to the trail head start. If you take the shuttle to the trail head you will be doing the Honolulu Ridge Trail and then the Mahana Ridge Trail to the visitors center and will go approximately 9.5 miles total but the back half along the Mahana Ridge Trail is mostly all down hill and gorgeous views.

If you decide to do all the the little spur hikes, it could be another mile added to your journey but it would be well worth it. The Uluhe Trail is .33 of a mile, Pine Loop Trail .10 of a mile, Pineapple Loop Trail .25 of a mile and the Akia Loop Trail if it is open. At the time we did the hike it was not maintained or passible.

Banyon Loop Trail

Directions

Distance:	1 mile
Elevation:	None to speak of
Trail:	Easy

From Lahaina go North on Honoapiilani Hwy. Turn left on Office Road. Then turn Right on Village Road and the Kapalua Adventure Center which is on the right. This is where you will start this trail.

This is an easy trail and gorgeous views from the lookout at the top of the trail. This hike is on private property at Kapalua and requires a free shuttle from Kapalua Village Center. Reservations are required because they only make 2 trips a day to the trailhead and seating is limited. This is a great thing because it makes the hike private and protects the surroundings and the trails by the limited access.

The trail is well maintained, marked and easy to follow. a narrow path, soft ground to hike on and a very slight elevation. There is a very detailed map at the beginning of the trail and a bathroom also. A great hike, beautiful trees, shade and great for the family also.

Kapalua Coastal Trail

Directions

Honapiilani Hwy towards Lahaina past Kaanapali to Coconut Grove Lane (mm29), turn left at the stoplight and go towards the ocean. Turn right at intersection, onto Lower Honoapiilani Rd, The sign is just past the Napili Kai Beach Resort.

Distance: 3 miles round trip
Elevation: None to speak of
Trail: Easy to moderate

This is a great coastal walk. This trail will take you from Kapalua Bay to DT Flemings Beach. You will pass by Oneloa Bay, Kapalua Bay Beach and end up at DT Flemings Beach. This is a beautiful coastal walk/hike, great for the entire family.

Good walking shoes are required even though most of the trail is paved there are some minor rocky spots. Little to no shade so make sure you have plenty of water and sunscreen on.

Oluwalu Cultural

Directions

From Lahaina go South on Honoapiilani Hwy 30 for approximately 6 miles to the Oluwalu General Store which is on the left side of the Hwy. Park in the lot and the trail begins behind the store.

Distance: 4 miles
Elevation: Minimal
Trail: Easy to Moderate
Amenities: No restrooms, there is a store, fruit stand and a restaurant.

The hike starts with you on a dirt road at the mouth of Oluwalu Valley. You will pass by several vegetable and herb farms and encounter many locals that live along the beginning of this trail. Be respectful and stay on the trail, these are people's yards and houses. This trail is well maintained with several stream crossings. More than 50% of the hike is in the shade. Don't blink because the petroglyphs are just around the corner and they are a unique sight for Maui. It is an easy hiking trail where water shoes or sneakers would be recommended. Don't forget plenty of water, sunscreen and you will need bug spray for this one also.

Lahaina Pali Trail

Directions

Distance:	6 miles
Elevation:	1600ft
Trail:	Moderate to Hard
Amenities:	There are none

The trailhead is on the inland side of the Honoapiilani Highway (30) between mile marker 10 and 11. It is 4 miles west of Ma'alaea Harbor and a half mile past the Lahaina tunnel coming from Kahului. There is a dirt pull out and parking for about 10-12 cars under some shade trees.

This provides gorgeous views and the climb of 1600ft is gradual yet steep in a couple of places. There are also switchbacks towards the top that makes the climb more manageable. The views from the top are beautiful and there always seems to be a breeze to make the no shade very comfortable.

Follow the same directions to start this trail as the Lahaina Pali trail on the next page. This hike will require two cars. One at the start of the trail and one at the end on the Ma'alaea side. You can start the trail from the Ma'alaea side but trust us when we say it is much better to end on that side.

This trail is not recommended for flip flops but tennis shoes will do just fine. When you reach the top you will be face to face with the giant windmills from Kaheawa Wind Farm. There is no shade or water. Start this hike early, bring lots of water and don't forget your sunscreen.

Lahaina Pali Trail

Directions

Distance:	3.5 miles
Elevation:	1600ft
Trail:	Moderate
Amenities:	No restrooms, no water

The trailhead is on the inland side of the kahekili Highway (30) between mile marker 10 and 11. It is 4 miles west of Ma'alaea Harbor and a half mile past the Lahaina Tunnel coming from Kahului. There is a dirt pull out and parking for about10-12 cars under some shade trees.

This is an old Hawaiian horse and foot trail in the early 1800's direct trail across the West Maui Mountains. It connects Lahaina and Olowalu with Ma'alaea and Wailuku. This trail offers gorgeous coastline shots of Lanai, Kahoolawe, Haleakala and Molokini Islands.

Start on the trail by walking thru the gate and up the steps onto the pavement until you come to the trailhead leading upwards to the left, there is a large arrow painted on the cement walkway to guide you when the trail starts up the side of the mountain. This provides gorgeous views and the climb of 1600ft is gradual yet steep in a couple of places. There are also switchbacks towards the top that makes the climb more manageable. The views from the top are beautiful and there always seemed to be a breeze to make the no shade very comfortable. This trail is not recommended for flip flops but tennis shoes will do just fine.

To extend this hike to a 6 mile adventure see the trail description on the previous page.

There is no shade or water. Start this hike early, bring lots of water and don't forget the sunscreen.

Wailea Boardwalk

Directions

From Kihei, take South Kihei road South until you reach Wailea Alanui Dr, turn right on Wailea Alanui Dr, and then right again on Kaukahi street. Follow this road to the end where there will be a parking lot on the right with a blue beach access sign.

Distance: 4 miles round trip
Elevation: none
Trail: Easy to moderate
Amenities: Restrooms, showers

This is a great hike along some of the most beautiful coastline in Maui. Wailea is the home to some the most world class resorts on the island. On a clear day you could be treated to sightings of the islands of Molokini, Kahoolawe and Lanai.

This is a great hike (or walk) that is mostly all concrete sidewalks. This is an easy to moderate 4 miles round trip. Great for the family but provides little to no shade. Make sure to bring water with you and use plenty of sunscreen. You are going to see five beaches along this walk; Keawakapu, Mokapu, Ulua, Wailea and Polo beaches.

La Perouse Bay

Directions

From Kihei go South on Hwy 31 until it turns slightly right and becomes Wailea Ike Dr. Turn left onto Wailea Alanui Dr and continue onto Makenna Rd. Take this to the end which is La Perouse Bay. Parking is limited.

Distance: 4 miles
Elevation: 67ft
Trail: Easy to Moderate
Amenities: Restroom in parking lot

You will be walking across 200 year old lava beds to a secluded beach. You will pass thru Kiawe Woodland and beaches with sand and white coral. When the vegetation stops it is a sign that you are on the newest of the lava beds, take a left turn thru the gate. The trail ends at Kanaio Beach where there should be a make shift swing made out of a log.

Parking is limited and there is no shade, so start this hike early. There are plenty of spots to get into the water, just don't go alone and be careful of your surroundings.

Waihou Spring Hike

Directions

Take Hwy 36/Hana Hwy to Hwy 37/Haleakala Hwy. Turn right to Makawoa Ave/State Rt 400. and turn left. At the intersection in town turn right onto Olinda Road. Stay on Olinda Road until you see a dirt parking lot on your right.

After parking, follow the wide trail to the first intersection; at this point you can go right or left and the trail is a short loop. There are side trails to check out that could extend your hike also.

Distance: 1.7 miles
Elevation: 584ft
Trail: Easy
Amenities: No restrooms

This is a well maintained easy walk trail with plenty of shade. Beautiful wooded area, easy trail to follow.

Makawao Forest

L O O P   T R A I L

Directions

Distance: 6.25
Elevation: 900ft
Trail: Easy (Moderate in very beginning)
Amenities: Restroom in the parking lot

From Kahului Take Hana Hwy to Hwy 37 and turn right. Then go to Makawao Ave and turn left, go thru town and then you will come to St Josephs Church, then turn right on Piiholo Rd and then left on Waiahiwi rd. There will be a fork in road, stay to the left which is still Waiahiwi rd and then turn right again when you come to Kahakapao Rd and then follow that up past a yellow gate and 4 speed bumps (that say dip) and into the parking lot.

The first 1/2 mile to the trailhead is a steep one but the beauty that awaits ahead is well worth the it. The trail lends itself to gentle breezes, plenty of shade and beautiful trees and plants. You will encounter Tropical Ash, Cook Pines and Eucalyptus trees. When you come to the trailhead and it gives you an option to go left or right, East Loop or West loop; go left on the East loop and come out the West loop.

When driving up the paved road to the parking lot you will cross a yellow gate and then 4 speed bumps about a 1/2 mile to the parking lot. When you come to the second yellow gate in the parking lot area go around the gate and walk 1/2 mile up to the beginning of the trail. There is plenty of shade, but again no water. Make sure you remember to bring water, sunscreen, and your camera. Tennis shoes or hiking boots are recommended. Might be a good idea to throw some rain gear in the car, this area is prone to last minute showers.

26

Boundary Trail

Directions

From Kahului: Head East on Hana Hwy 36 and then turn right on Haleakala Hwy 37 pass Pukalani. Approximately 14 miles to the second signed junction for Hwy 377. Turn left and then right on Waipoli Road. Continue up about 6 miles to the end of the pavement and then follow the unpaved road to the signed Boundary Trail which will be on the right.

Distance: 5.2 miles
Elevation: 850ft
Trail: Moderate to Strenuous
Amenities: No Amenities

This is a great trail that is made up of dirt and grass and pine needles. There are spectacular views, tons of birds and plenty of shade. There are two stream crossings, but no water in the streams when we went. You want to start this trail early as the clouds roll in the early afternoon. Still good for hiking but just harder to see.

Poli Poli State Park

Directions

From Kahului, take Highway 37 past Pukalani to the second turn for Hwy 377. Turn left on Hwy 377 for about .3 of a mile then turn right on Waipoli Rd. You will go about 6 miles on a paved windy road with gorgeous views of Central Maui and the West Maui Mountains. Then travel 4 more miles on an unpaved dirt road. Once you reach the sign to the right stating "Poli Poli Spring State Recreational Area" go to your right, thru the gate to the parking lot. If you blink you could miss the sign where you need to turn. If you get to the sign for the Haleakala Ridge Trail you have gone too far.

Distance: 5.5 miles
Elevation: 1500ft
Trail: Moderate to Strenuous
Amenities: Picnic tables, Camping, Lodging

A beautiful hike thru Redwood, Cedar and Ash trees. A well maintained trail that holds a different beauty around every corner. If you have a clear day take photos when you can because at any point the fog can role by or you can turn a corner and walk right into the clouds. There are gorgeous views and plenty of shade. The trails are well marked and we only encountered one down tree which we just went around and we were back on our way. You descend a 100 feet in the beginning which is an easy and constant down. There truly are wonders around every bend. Take the Redwood Trail, which starts by walking 300ft back up the road from the parking lot to the left by the yellow gate. Go thru the gate and the trailhead starts to the right of the cabin. From the Redwood Trail connect to the Tie Trail and then to the Plum Trail. There are several trails marked out there so check the marque at the beginning by the parking lot for the trail that best fits you.

Poli Poli State Park

Directions

From Kahului, take Hwy 37 past Pukalani to the second junction of Highway 377. Turn left on 377 for about 0.3 mile, then right on Waipoli Road. The road travels through the first cattle guard and climbs up the mountain through a long series of switchbacks.

Distance: 3 miles
Elevation: 600ft
Trail: Moderate to Strenuous
Amenities: No restrooms and only 2 parking spots

The trail starts by where you park at the hunter's check in station on the Poli Poli access road. You walk thru the gate, then walk about 0.8 of a mile to the beginning of the trail and go thru another gate, make sure to close this gate behind you. When you come to a split in the trail take the right side, you will come out on the left. There is a slight incline at the beginning and at the end of this trail.

The trail is well maintained and parts of the trail are wide enough for 2 people although most of the trail is only wide enough for one person at a time. There are some rocky areas, that if wet, could be slippery. The trail is lined with pine needles and has a very soft feel. You are walking thru the Kula Forrest and the scenery is varied of pine trees and timberland trees.

Haleakala Ridge Trail

Directions

From Kahului, take Highway 37 past Pukalani to the second turn for Hwy 377. Turn left on Hwy 377 for about .3 of a mile then turn right on Waipoli Rd. Follow Waipoli Rd approximately another 6 miles to the end of the pavement. Then another 3.5 miles on the unpaved road until the road splits, take the right fork for about a half a mile as it heads down to the campground and parking area at the end of the road.

Distance:	3.2 miles round trip
Elevation:	850ft
Trail:	Easy to moderate
Amenities:	Restrooms and picnic tables

To begin, take the signed Poli Poli trail to the right, if facing the campground area. You will come to a junction in the trail about a half a mile in. Take the left fork this will lead you to the Haleakala Ridge Trail. Take another left fork when the trail intersects with the Skyline Road. This trail will be heading down on the Waipoli Rd. When he road splits again go left again, down hill towards the campground.

You can also start this trail by continuing up the road and not going down to the camp grounds. If you do this look for the guard rail and the sign pictured on the next page. If you start here you will hike down until you come to the fork in road and you will stay straight until you come to a sign that says Plum Trail. Here you will have reached the end of the trail and you will need to turn around and climb back out to get to where you parked your car. Either way you go, there are some spectacular views.

This trail is well maintained and is a well marked dirt road. On a clear day it offers great views of Mauna Kea and Mauna Loa. Two of the more spectacular volcanoes on the Island of Hawaii.

Halemauu Trail

Directions

Distance: 7.8 miles
Elevation: 1030ft loss and gain
Trail: Strenuous to Difficult (because of elevation)
Amenities: Restrooms at parking lot area

From Kahului, take Hwy 37 to Hwy 377 then to Hwy 378. Halemauu Trail is approximately14.2 miles up Hwy 378. You will see a parking lot for this trail.

Talk about a beautiful hike. This trail starts at 7990ft elevation and takes you to the bottom floor of Haleakala. A rocky, well maintained trail that requires hiking boots or sneakers. This is not a trail for flip flops. The elevation gain out is moderate because of the switchbacks, they make the climb out not seem like that much of a climb. Easy compared to the climb out that you encounter on the sliding sands trail.

From the top of the trail the lava formations on the bottom look as if the lava is still flowing. The way the rocks have settled in a perfect flowing pattern makes for a beautiful illusion. At the bottom of the trail there is a gate you go thru that leads you into the wonder of the bottom of the volcano floor. Not at all what you would expect, there is lush green foliage waist high with glorious colors and lava dust and gravel cones that will amaze you.

If you plan to hike from one end to the other, then our suggestion would be to go down Sliding Sands Trail across the bottom and then back up the Halemauu Trail. This trail is amazing and you will not be disappointed.

Sliding Sands Trail

Directions

From Kahului, take Hana Hwy (36) SE past the airport turnoff then turn right onto Haleakala Hwy (37) go about 8 miles then turn left and continue on Haleakala Hwy 377. After about 6 more miles going towards Kula turn left on Hwy 378 which becomes Crater Rd. Continue uphill and after stopping at the rangers station, at the beginning of the park and paying the fee, you have about 5 more miles to go. You know you are there when you get to the giant parking lot just before the sign that has you continue to the summit. Park and gather your stuff the trail starts just right of the end of the parking lot. You will see a sign and a lava rock path that leads to the right and curves around to the left and you are on your way to some of the most spectacular views you have ever seen.

Distance: 6.5 miles
Elevation: 2200 ft Decline
Trail: Strenuous
Amenities: Picnic tables, restrooms and public telephones

The trail is very well maintained and is an easy to moderate walk. There are parts even wide enough for 2 people to walk side by side. Lava sand makes up most of the trail. The trail is strenuous because of the incline when hiking back out. Be careful this trail is a walk in the park when descending into the volcano but always remember what goes down must come out.

The views are spectacular and the clouds are awesome. Around every corner a different view. The overall hike is well worth the effort. Even if you only hike in a little ways and then back out, you will not be disappointed. Remember to dress warm and in layers. Wear hiking boots, not the place for flip flops. Bring water and make sure you have a rain jacket or dry clothes in the car for after the hike in case that it rains. The weather is always unpredictable.

38

Waianapanapa Coastal

Directions

From Kahului, take Hana Hwy 36 approximately 53 miles to Waianapanapa State Park. It will be signed. Turn left and park in lot.

Distance: 3 miles
Elevation: None to speak of
Trail: Easy to Moderate
Amenities: Restrooms, picnic area, vending and showers.

This trail starts at Waianapanapa State Park, this trail is Kings Highway North. Kings Highway South starts at the park also. This trail is also called Kipapa O Kihapi'ilani Trail. This trail is easy but rugged, meaning tennis shoes or hiking boots are recommended. This is a lava rock trail (as seen in the photo) with some spots of a lava sand. Bring water there is very little shade. Gorgeous coastal views, sea cliffs and blow holes. Boulder Beach is about 1.8 miles in and is just that. A beautiful beach but all boulders, hence the name.

The path is easily marked and not difficult to follow. It ends at the fence for Hana Airport. You will see a red flag that marks the airport, don't sneeze because you could miss it on the left. Stay off the runway, this is a real airport and trespassing is a federal offense and a terrible way to end a vacation.

Enjoy the scenery, take lots of photos and turn around at the airport and head back in, maybe take a dip in the waters at Black Sand Beach when you get back.

Waianapanapa Coastal

Directions

From Kahului take Highway 36 approximately 53 miles to Waianapanapa State Park. It will be signed. Turn left and park in the parking lot.

Distance: 4.5 miles
Elevation: None to speak of
Trail: Easy to Moderate
Amenities: Restrooms, picnic area, vending and showers.

This trail starts at Waianapanapa State Park, this trail is Kings Highway South. Kings Highway North starts at this park also. There is really no elevation gain to speak of as most of the trail is made up of small lava rocks and palm leaves. The trail starts out on the pavement and then transcends to lava as you make your way down the coast. The trail passes blow holes, sea arches, tide pools and beautiful coastal scenery.

The path is easily marked and ends when you pass a small hand made fisherman's shed and a sign just past that says Hana Bay 2 miles. You could continue two more miles to Hana Bay or for this trail just turn around and return back the same way you came.

Pipiwai Trail

Directions

From Kahului take Hana Hwy 36 to 360 to 31. Park in the parking lot. This is considered Kapahulu Area (Coastal). The park where the parking lot and restrooms are actually in the Haleakala National Park area. Fees are required to park there

Distance:	4 miles
Elevation:	900ft
Trail:	Moderate to Difficult
Amenities:	Parking, restrooms and a picnic area. All located in Haleakala.

Waimoku Falls is a spectacular 400ft waterfall with a great pool to swim in when the falls are flowing good. The trail is located at the end of Hana Highway in the Kipahulu are of Haleakala National Park, starting at the visitors center.

There are a couple of other falls you will encounter along the way, depending on the rain fall and weather conditions. One is Makahiku Falls, a 180ft waterfall from one of the trails overlooks. The trail continues along the stream, passes over 2 bridges and past some beautiful Banyon trees before making your way onto a wood plank pathway that guides you thru a magnificent bamboo forest. As the Bamboo forest opens up at the end of the trail here is where you will be greeted with a beautiful 400ft waterfall. The first 30 minutes of the trail there is a steep incline and then it levels off with only a few more moderate inclines as you make your way.

Iao Valley

Directions

From Kahului take Hwy 380/Keolani pl slight right onto Hwy 36A. Then a slight left onto E Kaahumanu Ave and continue onto Main St. Keep right to Iao Valley Rd.

Distance:	2.5 miles
Elevation:	200ft
Trail:	Easy to Moderate
Amenities:	Restrooms in parking lot

This is a peaceful 4,000 acre, 10 mile long park, with the landmark Iao Needle towering above. This trail is for hiking boots or sneakers, not recommended for slippers or flip flops.

To start the trail, walk thru the park up to the lookout for Iao Needle. There will be a railing there to the left of the house-like structure, when you look over the railing you will see the trail. Climb over the railing and you are on your way. You can go as far as you like on this trail, just remember that this is not a loop trail, however far you go in you have to come back out.

Waihe'e Coastal Dunes

Directions

Distance: 3 miles
Elevation: None to speak of
Trail: Easy
Amenities: Restrooms and picnic tables

From Kaahumanu Ave. in Kahului turn right on Kahului Beach Rd. Turn right onto Hwy 340/Waiehu Beach Rd. Continue to follow Hwy 340 onto Halewaiu Rd. Turn left to the parking lot for Waihe'e Coastal Dunes and Wetlands Refuge.

This is an easy, dirt path and a flat wetland trail. You start the trail by walking thru a small gate. When you see the sign for the golf course veer to the left from the parking lot. There is a trail to the right as well but this trail is not scenic at all, it is much better to go in on the left and come back out the same way. This is a quiet and picturesque hike and is just East of the longest and widest reefs on Maui. You will need sunscreen and bug spray, especially after rainfall.

48

Waihee Ridge Trail

Distance:	5 miles
Elevation:	1560ft
Trail:	Strenuous
Amenities:	Restrooms in parking lot

Directions

Take Highway 32 West from Kahului to Highway 330 about 3 miles. Then turn right on highway 330 and continue until it becomes highway 240 at 9/10 of a mile past mile marker 6 is the Malaria Boy Scout Camp on the left. Turn left here and about one mile up the hill until you reach a small parking lot.

From the parking lot you start the trail by passing thru a cattle proof gate and then up 200ft on a cement road that is far steeper than it looks. A beautiful trail that passes by Kukui, Guava, Chia and plenty of ferns. If you are lucky and the water is flowing you should be able to see Makamaka'ole Falls from a distance.

Sneakers are fine for this trail and you need to start early because of the potential weather and clouds that can appear out of no where. There is some shade but mostly open areas. By far, one of our favorite hikes of all on Maui, just for the sheer beauty of the area.

Makamakaole Stream

Distance:	2.5 miles
Elevation:	813ft
Trail:	Easy
Amenities:	No restrooms, parking for about 9 cars

Directions

From Kahului, take Kahului Beach Road until you get to Waiehu Beach Road and then turn right. Then go until you hit Hwy 340 and turn right. Then go just past mile marker 7 and the trailhead starts by the wooden post.

It is called "13 Stream Crossing" for a reason and if you count them as you travel along this trail you will find that indeed there are 13. You will pass guava trees, bamboo trees, jobe's tears plants and a lot of ferns. After the 11th crossing there will be a fork at the stream, stay to the right.

At the end of the trail is a beautiful 40ft waterfall with a nice pool for swimming. Well worth the hike and a great added bonus. There used to be a rope, that after you take a very short but very steep climb to the right of the falls you could climb over and up to another fall. At the time that we did this hike the rope was not there.

Most of the entire trail is in the shade but there are parts where the sun peaks thru. Don't forget sunscreen, bug spray, water shoes and of course water. Not a trail for flip flops.

Kahakuloa Hike

Directions

From Kahului, take Hwy 340 North to Kahakuloa, approximately 14.5 miles and 45 minutes without traffic.

You can also come from Lahaina, via Hwy 30 North past Kapalua, keep going and you will connect into Hwy 340. Approximately 23.5 miles and one hour drive, again with no traffic.

Distance: 8 miles round trip
Elevation: 1400ft
Trail: Difficult
Amenities: None

Located in the West Maui Forest Reserve. This is a well maintained trail located on a hunters road called Waikalai. The trail starts out by passing thru 2 gates and is not passible if wet or if it has rained.

You will pass by Guava and Pine trees. Little or no shade exists so bring lots of water and sunscreen. This trail offers gorgeous vista and scenic views of the valley.

The directions give you two ways to come from. Both very scenic and pretty equal in time.

Kahekili Hwy

Directions

Distance: 0.6 miles
Elevation: 225ft
Trail: Easy to Moderate
Amenities: No Restrooms

From Kahului take Kaahumanu Avenue .3 of a mile. Turn right on Kahalui Beach Rd, and go 1.2 miles then turn right on Highway 340/Waiehu Beach Rd. Follow Highway 340 for approximately 14.9 miles to around mile marker 16 and parking is on the right.

From Lahaina; take Highway 30 past Kaanapali, Kapalua and DT Fleming Beach. Keep following the highway around and parking will be on the left. About 21 miles and 47 minutes if no traffic.

This is a well maintained easy to follow hike. The trail does veer off to the right or left and you want to stay left.

Great views of the baths, you will want to go early because there are many visitors and the pools become full and crowded.

Ohai Loop Trail

Directions

From Lahaina go North on Honoapiilani Hwy (Hwy 30) The trail is between mile marker 40 and 41.

Distance: 1.5 miles
Elevation: 200ft
Trail: Easy
Amenities: No restrooms

This is an easy walking trail with beautiful coastal views. There is a vista overlook but don't stop there, take the dirt path to the right and do this great little trail. There are informative nature signs alone the trail and again spectacular views. This is a great hike for families and kids, a must do.

Upper Puaaluu Falls/On the road to Hana/mm 43

60

Bamboo Forest/Waimoku Falls Trail/Hana Area

Haleakala/Sliding Sands Trail

Pua'a-Lu'u Falls/On the road to Hana/mm 43

Red Sand Beach/On the road to Hana

Three Bears Waterfall/Road to Hana/mm 19

Alelele Falls/Road to Hana/mm 39

GUIDE TO WATERFALLS

1. Twin Falls
2. Twin Falls
3. Twin Falls
4. Twin Falls
5. Twin Falls
6. Na'ili'ili-Haele Falls
7. Na'ili'ili-Haele Falls
8. Na'ili'ili-Haele Falls
9. Waikamoi Falls
10. Upper Waikamoi Falls
11. Lower Waikamoi Falls
12. Lower Puohokamoa Falls
13. Upper Puohokamoa Falls
14. Haipua'ena Falls
15. Punalau Falls
16. Chings Pond
17. Upper Waikani Falls
18. Wailua Iki Falls

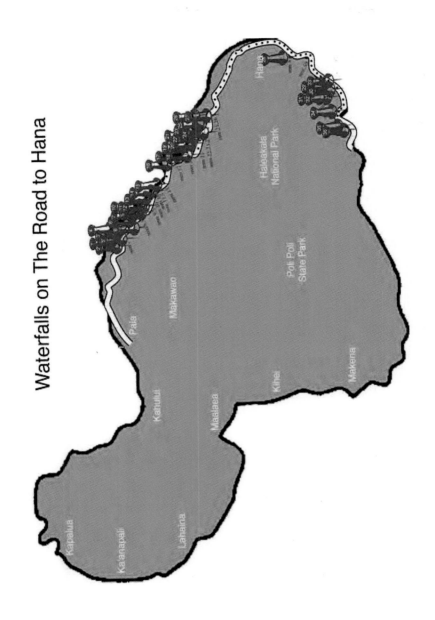

Waterfalls on The Road to Hana

Twin Falls

Location:

At mm 2 at the beginning of Hana Hwy.

There are several small falls at this location, a fruit stand that is usually open and restrooms available. To get to Twin Falls it does require a short hike in where you can venture off to each side of the trail and witness several other falls. An easy hike, that most family members can easily do.

Mile Marker 2

70

Twin Falls Area

At mm 2 at the beginning of Hana Hwy.

There are several small falls at this location, a fruit stand that is usually open and restrooms available. There are several small paths that lead to some very pretty quaint falls that are pictured in the following pages labeled Twin Falls Area.

Mile Marker 2

72

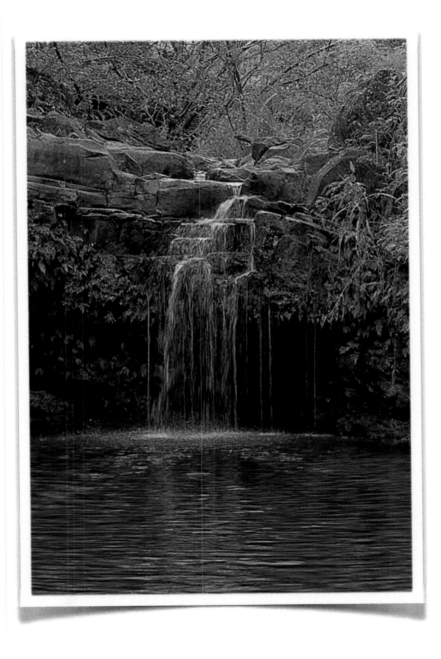

73

Twin Falls Area

At mm 2 at the beginning of Hana Hwy.

There are several small falls at this location, a fruit stand that is usually open and restrooms available. There are several small paths that lead to some very pretty quaint falls that are pictured in the following pages labeled Twin Falls Area.

Mile Marker 2

Twin Falls Area

There are several small falls at this location, a fruit stand that is usually open and restrooms available. There are several small paths that lead to some very pretty quaint falls that are pictured in the following pages labeled Twin Falls Area.

Mile Marker 2

Twin Falls Area

At mm 2 at the beginning of Hana Hwy.

There are several small falls at this location, a fruit stand that is usually open and restrooms available. There are several small paths that lead to some very pretty quaint falls that are pictured in the following pages labeled Twin Falls Area.

Mile Marker 2

Na'ili'ili-Haele

Just pass mm 6 at 6.5 there is parking on the left and the right, go thru the fence and the trail is on the right. You will be hiking thru a bamboo forest and the path can be impassible if after a heavy rain. There are four falls along this trail, the photo to the right is the 1st one that is often missed by many. There will be some wall climbing with a rope (not as bad as it sounds, rather easy) and a ladder to climb up to the short hike for the last fall and also to get the last falls you will need to do a little swimming, so be prepared to get wet.

Mile Marker 6.5

81

Na'ili'ili-Haele Falls

Location:

1/2 mile past mm 6 on Hana Hwy. Ranging from 15 to 50ft in size.

Just pass mm 6 at 6.5 there is parking on the left and the right, go thru the fence and the trail is on the right. You will be hiking thru a bamboo forest and the path can be impassible if after a heavy rain. There are four falls alone this trail, the photo to the right is the 2nd one. There will be some wall climbing with a rope (not as bad as it sounds, rather easy) and a ladder to climb up to the short hike for the last fall and also to get the last falls you will need to do a little swimming, so be prepared to get wet. This is the second falls that you come to. Ready to climb the rope and the wall?

Mile Marker 6.5

Na'ili'ili-Haele Falls

Location:

1/2 mile past mm 6 on Hana Hwy. Ranging from 15 to 50ft in size.

Just pass mm 6 at 6.5 there is parking on the left and the right, go thru the fence and the trail is on the right. You will be hiking thru a bamboo forest and the path can be impassible if after a heavy rain. There are four falls alone this trail, the photo to the right is the 3rd one. There will be some wall climbing with a rope (not as bad as it sounds, rather easy) and a ladder to climb up to the short hike for the last fall and also to get the last falls you will need to do a little swimming, so be prepared to get wet. This is the third falls that you come to. Next is the ladder, pretty steep but easy enough.

Mile Marker 6.5

Lower Waikamoi Falls

Location:

1/2 mile past mm 9 on Hana Hwy. A 30ft waterfall.

When the water is flowing, this is a beautiful waterfall with a great swimming pool area. A short path to a great hidden falls. If the water is low than it could be just a trickle, but still a great place to take a dip when its hot outside.

Mile Marker 9.5

Waikamoi Falls Area

This waterfall is located at the area that is marked the Waikamoi Nature Trail. The trail itself is a great little hike for families and children. It is at the end of the trail that there is a sign that is marked end of trail. If you continue past this trail and take the path that leads down to the left, you will come to a viaduct area, this can be tricky and is not recommended for children or anyone else for that matter that is not completely comfortable with scrambling down the side of the viaduct and then across the wall. If you are game and the water is not flowing very strong it is passable. You will need to climb down the side, walk across the wall area and then get your feet wet as you walk up the stream. Trust me when I tell you no matter how the water is flowing the rocks are very very slippery and many people fall all the time. So even though there are (2) waterfalls in this area you might want to pass for safety reasons. This is the first of the two falls that you will see.

Mile Marker 9.5

89

Upper Waikamoi Falls

Location:

mm9.5 on Hana Hwy.

This waterfall is located at the are that is marked the Waikamoi Nature Trail. The trail itself is a great little hike for families and children. It is at the end of the trail that there is a sign that is marked end of trail. If you continue past this trail and take the path that leads down to the left, you will come to a viaduct area, this can be tricky and is not recommended for children or anyone else for that matter that is not completely comfortable with scrambling down the side of the viaduct and then across the wall. If you are game and the water is not flowing very strong it is passable. You will need to climb down the side, walk across the wall area and then get your feet wet as you walk up the stream. Trust me when I tell you no matter how the water is flowing the rocks are very very slippery and many people fall all the time. So even though there are (2) waterfalls in this area you might want to pass for safety reasons. This is the second falls that you will see.

Mile Marker 9.5

Lower Puohokamoa

Location:

.8 mile past mm10 on Hana Hwy. A 160ft waterfall.

You have to view this falls before the Upper Puohokamoa. Most miss this falls due to it being hidden out of the way. The pull out is .8 of a mile past mm 10 near a telephone pole. There is a path by a fence that leads to the view of Lower Puohokamoa.

Mile Marker 10

Upper Puohokamoa

Location:

mm 11 on Hana Hwy.
A 30ft waterfall.

There is a bridge and a small parking space on the mauka side. There is a short path that leads to the falls and a small pool. There is possibly a land dispute going on and there may be a fence and a locked gate blocking the path when you get there.

Mile Marker 11

Haipua'ena Falls

1/2 mile past mm 11 on Hana Hwy. A 30ft waterfall.

This is a small falls, but very pretty. A short walk to a refreshing pool. A great place to cool off. There is a short trail next to the bridge, maybe 5 minutes off of the road that leads to this falls. Because you can not see it from the road, most pass it by and don't even stop. It's worth it if you love waterfalls to stop.

Mile Marker 11.5

Punalau Falls

Location:

*1/4 mile past mm13
on Hana Hwy.*

Requires you to boulder hop,
approximately 800ft upstream.
The rocks can be slippery
depending on the rain fall but
take your time it is well worth the
adventure.

Mile Marker 13

Chings Pond

At mm 17 on Hana Hwy.

There is a path approximately 75ft to the left that leads you to the pool. If you park by the Hunter's Road, Piinaau Road on the right before the bridge, directly across from that road is the path that leads you to the base of this falls.

Mile Marker 17

Upper Waikani Falls

Location:

Between mm 19&20 on Hana Hwy.

Better known as Three Bears Falls. One of the most beautiful falls on the road to Hana and one of the most popular. There is almost no parking, just a small pullout before the bridge. You can park farther up the road and walk back down, but please be careful walking on the road. There is a small trail to the left and the right of the falls that can take you down to the bottom of the falls. The trail on the left is the better trail but still sketchy when the ground is wet. Use caution if you go to the bottom, otherwise the view from the bridge is terrific.

Mile Marker 19&20

Wailua Iki Falls

mm 21 on Hana Hwy.

At mm 21 there is a small pullout just in front of a sign for a Hunter's Road called Wailua Iki Rd. After you go around the gate, approximately 1/4 mile or about 20 minutes up the road you will come to the first waterfall off to the right. When it is flowing you can see what is pictured on this page. We have seen this waterfall at just a trickle and at any flow it is a pretty sight coming right out of the side of the cliff.

Mile Marker 21

Wailua Iki Falls

At mm 21 there is a small pullout just in front of a sign for a hunter's road called Wailua Iki Rd. After you go around the gate, approximately 1/4 mile or about 20 minutes up the road you will come to the first waterfall off to the right. Now go past this waterfall about 100 yards or so, cross over the bridge and there is a beautiful pool at its base but not suitable for swimming. We found no way to get into the pool and the unknown is not worth the risk more often than not.

Mile Marker 21

Wailua Iki Falls

At the bridge there is parking for really only one vehicle and the falls requires a walk up the road and then look back to see the full falls. Just be careful, as mentioned elsewhere in the book, when walking on the roadway to watch out for the other vehicles.

Mile Marker 21

Unknown Waterfalls

Along Hana Hwy

Along the Hana Hwy there are many waterfalls that appear and disappear throughout the year. Depending on the weather and EMI water diversion going on. There are also many that are always there just hidden or more difficult to get to than the average person should explore. Even though you may or not be able to see these or find these in your travels we felt they were beautiful and important enough to include them; so here they are, we hope that you get to see them and if not enjoy the possibility thru the photographs on the next few pages.

Along Hana Hwy

Unknown Waterfalls

Along Hana Hwy

Along the Hana Hwy there are many waterfalls that appear and disappear throughout the year, depending on the weather and EMI water diversion going on. There are also many that are always there just hidden or more difficult to get to than the average person should explore. Even though you may or not be able to see these or find these in your travels we felt they were beautiful and important enough to include them; so here they are, we hope that you get to see them and if not enjoy the possibility thru the photographs on the next few pages.

Along Hana Hwy

Waiokamilo Falls

Along Hana Hwy

Along the Hana Hwy there are many waterfalls that appear and disappear throughout the year. Depending on the weather and EMI water diversion going on. There are also many that are always there just hidden or more difficult to get to than the average person should explore. Even though you may or not be able to see these or find these in your travels we felt they were beautiful and important enough to include them; so here they are, we hope that you get to see them and if not enjoy the possibility thru the photographs on the next few pages. This waterfall is tucked in the Ko'olua Forest Reserve, falling 200ft below a bridge that was built in 1922. It is a primitive, almost untouched, a vast open area filled with lush greenery and gorgeous views of the valley that surrounds.

Ko'olau Forest Reserve

Pua'a Ka'a Lower Falls

Location:

Between mm 22 & 23 on Hana Hwy

Between mm 22&23 there is a wayside park called Pua'a Ka'a. There are restrooms here and parking at the restroom area. Across the street is the park where you will find two small but very pretty falls just off of the road. If you go up the hill, following the sidewalk in the park area, you will need to make a brief and fairly easy stream crossing and you will come to a larger falls and a pool area that you can swim in. After crossing the stream you will see a path that is steep and usually very muddy and slippery that leads uphill to the right. There is another larger falls at the top. Every time that we have been there, we were not able to do this. If you are able, be careful and remember as hard as it is to get up there trail it will be even harder coming down.

Mile Marker 22 & 23

Pua'a Ka'a Lower Falls

Location:

Between mm 22 & 23
on Hana Hwy

Between mm 22&23 there is a wayside park called Pua'a Ka'a. There are restrooms here and parking at the restroom area. Across the street is the park where you will find two small but very pretty falls just off of the road. If you go up the hill, following the sidewalk in the park area, you will need to make a brief and fairly easy stream crossing and you will come to a larger falls and a pool area that you can swim in. After crossing the stream you will see a path that is steep and usually very muddy and slippery that leads uphill to the right. There is another larger falls at the top. Every time that we have been there, we were not able to do this. If you are able, be careful and remember as hard as it is to get up there trail it will be even harder coming down.

Mile Marker 22 & 23

Hanawi Falls

Between mm 23 and 24 on Hana Hwy.

Between mm 23 and mm 24 at the bridge there is a pretty waterfall on the right and if the water is flowing good, after a rain storm there is another waterfall on the left side. We have only seen it flowing once in the past 12 years. This one pictured here can be seen on the right side.

Mile Marker 23 & 24

Hanawi Falls

Between mm 23 and 24 on Hana Hwy

Between mm 23 and mm 24 at the bridge there is a pretty waterfall on the right and if the water is flowing good, after a rain storm there is another waterfall on the left side. We have only seen it flowing once in the past 12 years. This one pictured here can be seen on the left side.

Mile Marker 23 & 24

122

Makapipi Falls

Location:

*Between mm 25 & 26
on Hana Hwy.*

Park at the bridge and then walk up the road about 100 yards. Then turn around and look back. If you are not too squeamish you will need to get close to the edge to get this angle for a photo. A very pretty waterfall and at least worth the stop. If you are not looking for this one you will drive over the bridge and pass this one by.

Mile Marker 25 & 26

Paihi Falls

Location:

At mm 45 on Hana Hwy.

This falls is between mm 44 and 45. There is little place to park and it is hard to get a photo of this pretty falls. This is a very pretty 50ft waterfall.

Mile Marker 45

Hahalawa Gulch Falls

Location:

At mm 43 on the Hana Hwy.

Off of the Hahalawa Stream there is a steep path just past the bridge that leads you to the bottom of these falls.

Mile Marker 43

Pua'a-Lu'u Falls

Location:

At mm 43 on Hana Hwy.

After you pass over the bridge there is a little pullout. Cross the road and there is a path that takes you to the bottom of the falls. This trail can be muddy and slippery so be careful. Also make sure you have mosquito repellent.

Mile Marker 43

Seven Sacred Pools

Location:

Parking is at mm 39 on the Hana Hwy at the Haleakala National Park.

Parking is at The Haleakala National Park. Walk down the parking lot and there is a small trail that will take you to the pools. Be aware this is a very popular place and not a place to swim alone.

Mile Marker 39

133

Unknown Falls

Location:

At mm 42 on the Hana Hwy while hiking the Pipiwai Trail.

This is one of the two smaller waterfalls you will see while hiking the Pipiwai Trail on your way to Waimoku Falls. This one is about 2/3 of a mile in on the trail and is a beautiful 200ft drop. Different times of the year produce different amounts of water flow, so don't be surprised if there might be less water than pictured here when you pass by.

Mile Marker 42

Waimoku Falls

Location:

At mm 42 on Hana Hwy.

You will hike 2 miles on the trail known as Pipiwai Trail. You will park in the parking lot at Haleakala National Park and then will cross the road and start the trail. The trail will take you in and out of the trees, past (2) distant falls that can easily be seen when they are flowing. There is a small incline in the beginning, you will cross over two bridges hike thru a remarkable bamboo forest. At the end of the trail you will be treated with a beautiful 400t waterfall. The largest waterfall on Maui that you have access to.

Mile Marker 42

137

Alelele Falls

At mm 39 on Hana Hwy.

Parking is at the Alelele Bridge and then it is a short hike. Boulder hoping and your feet will get wet, but the hike is easy and well worth it. At the end is a beautiful 245ft waterfall, in a secluded area with a nice pool for swimming. Most of the time you will have this falls to yourself. Enjoy.

Mile Marker 39

139

Unknown Waterfalls

Location:

Along Hana Hwy

Along the Hana Hwy there are many waterfalls that appear and disappear throughout the year. Depending on the weather and EMI water diversion going on. There are also many that are always there just hidden or more difficult to get to than the average tourists should explore. Even though you may or not be able to see these or find these in your travels we felt they were beautiful and important enough to include them; so here they are, we hope that you get to see them and if not enjoy the possibility thru the photographs on the next few pages.

Along Hana Hwy

Unknown Waterfalls

Location:

Along Hana Hwy

Along the Hana Hwy there are many waterfalls that appear and disappear throughout the year. Depending on the weather and EMI water diversion going on. There are also many that are always there just hidden or more difficult to get to than the average tourists should explore. Even though you may or not be able to see these or find these in your travels we felt they were beautiful and important enough to include them; so here they are, we hope that you get to see them and if not enjoy the possibility thru the photographs on the next few pages.

Along Hana Hwy

Iao Valley

Kaanapali Beach

Honolulu Ridge Trail

Poli Poli State Park

DT Fleming Beach

GUIDE TO BEACHES

31. Kama'ole III
32. Keawakapu Beach
33. Mokapu Beach
34. Ulua Beach
35. Wailea Beach
36. Polo Beach
37. White Rock Beach
38. Secrets Beach
39. Po'Olenalena Beach
40. Makena Landing
41. Malu'aka Beach
42. Black Sand Beach
43. Little Beach
44. Big Beach
45. Secret Secret Beach
46. Hamoa Beach
47. Koki Beach
48. Red Sand Beach
49. Hana Beach Park
50. Black Sand Beach
51. Ho'okipa Beach Park
52. Mama's Fish House
53. Tavares Bay Beach
54. Paia Bay Beach
55. Secret Beach (Paia)
56. H.A. Baldwin Beach
57. Spreckelsville Beach
58. Kanaha Beach
59. Kahului Beach Harbor
60. Kite Beach
61. Waihee Beach Park

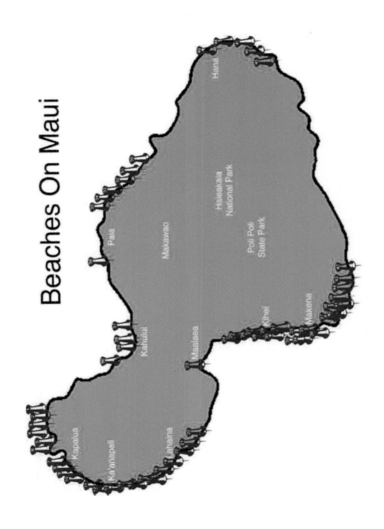

Beaches On Maui

Windmills Beach

Location:

Go North on Honoapiilani Hwy past Honoloa Bay to mile marker 34.5. You will see a turnoff to the park.

Amenities: Swimming

A sandy and rocky beach, a great place for a walk on the beach. Often secluded and very peaceful. Also known as Punalau Beach.

Upper West

Honolua Bay

Location:

From Lahaina take Honoapiilani Hwy 30 Northbound, between mile marker 31-32.

Amenities: Swimming and snorkeling.

Marine life Conservation District, no fishing is allowed here, ensuring the sea life will forever flourish. Some say the North point of the beach is where you will find the perfect wave.

Kapalua/Upper West

Slaughterhouse Beach

Location:

Off of Honoapiilani Hwy at mile marker 32.

Amenities: Swimming and snorkeling.

Also known as Mokule'ia Beach in the Honolua area. There was actually a slaughterhouse built here and tore down in the 60's. This hidden gem is a secluded white sand beach. You have to climb down approximately 87 steps to get to this beach but it is well worth it.

Upper West Maui

DT Fleming Beach

Location:

North of Kapalua, on Hwy 30 around mile marker 31.

Amenities: Restrooms, picnic area, swimming, snorkeling, showers and life guards.

Great for swimming and surfing. This beach was named after D.T. Fleming, the man who introduced pineapple to West Maui.

Kapalua/Upper West

Oneloa Beach

Location:

Off of Honoapiilani Hwy between mile markers 31-32, left on office road, left on Lower Honoapiilani rd, right on Ridge Road, then right on Ironwood Lane.

Amenities: Swimming and snorkeling.

Also called Ironwoods Beach. 1/4 mile long, sits next to the Ritz Carlton Resort.

Kapalua/Upper West

Kapalua Bay Beach

Location:

Off of Honoapiilani Hwy 30 and Napilihau St. Parking is just past Napili Kai Beach Resort.

Amenities: Restrooms, swimming, snorkeling and showers.

The reef is shallow, great for divers. One of the most beautiful beaches on the island.

Kapalua/Upper West

Napili Bay Beach

Location:

Off of Lower Honoapiilani Road and Napilihau St. On Hui Road park along roadside.

Amenities: Swimming and snorkeling.

Monk seals have made this beach their home.
Beautiful white sand beach.

Napili/Upper West

Kahana Beach

Location:

Off of Lower Honoapiilani Hwy from Lahaina, North of Pohahu Park. Left on Hoohui Rd and park at Kahana Beach Resort.

Amenities: Swimming, snorkeling, windsurfing and

This is a great beach for windsurfers. This is a sandy beach when the surf is up you need to be careful because of the rocks can make it difficult for swimming.

Kahana/Upper West

Keone Nui Beach

Amenities: Snorkeling

Location:

Off of Honoapiilani Hwy at mile marker 29.

Located at the Kahana Sunset, where they have almost claimed the beach as their own. This is not a private beach. All beaches on the island have public access regardless of what others may say. Enjoy and happy snorkeling.

Kahana/Upper West

Honokowai Beach

Location:

Between mile marker 25 and 26 off of Lower Honoapiiliani Hwy.

Amenities: Restrooms, picnic areas, swimming, snorkeling and showers.

This is a community local beach, great for families and kids. It has a swing set and large grassy area. This is a very shallow calm area and provides good snorkeling beyond the reef area.

Ka'anapali/Upper West

Kahekili Beach

Amenities: Restrooms, picnic areas, swimming, snorkeling and showers.

Off of Honoapiilani Hwy 30, turn left at Kai Ala Dr/Puukolii Rd and follow straight into parking lot.

Great beach, soft sand and very popular. To get a good spot go early as this beach fills up fast. Each little cove has great things to explore and this one is no exception. The snorkeling is good and this is a great beach to bring the kids.

Ka'anapali/Upper West

Ka'anapali Beach

Location:

Off of Hwy 30, past Lahaina.

Amenities: Swimming, snorkeling and showers.

Brave jumpers love this beach for its high volcanic ocean cliff. In the middle of the beach is a place called Black Rock. Great for snorkeling, abundant coral and bright tropical fish. Nice three mile stretch beach.

Ka'anapali/Upper West

Hanakao'o Beach

Location:

Off of Honoapiilani Hwy 30, between mile marker 23 & 24.

Amenities: Restrooms, picnic area, swimming, snorkeling and lifeguards.

Also known as Canoe Beach. Right at the South end of Ka'anapali Beach. Great area for jet skis and canoes.

Ka'anapali/Upper West

Wahikuli Beach

Location:

Off of Honoapiilani Hwy 30 North and it will be by mile marker 23.

Amenities: Restrooms, picnic areas, swimming, snorkeling and showers.

Wahikuli means noisy place. This beach sits right off of the highway. It is a great spot for snorkeling and just off the shore the water drops off quickly so not a great spot for kids to swim.

Lahaina/West Maui

Mala Beach

Location:

Off of Front Street and Ala Moana Street at the end.

Amenities: Restrooms and swimming.

Better area for surfers and fisherman, swimming is possible but can get a little sketchy when big waves are coming in.

Lahaina/West Maui

Pu'unoa Beach

Amenities: None

Location:

Off of Front Street, You can access the beach by parking at the intersection of Kai Pali Place & Kamaka Circle.

Also known as Baby Beach in Lahaina. This beach is well protected from the winds and makes it a great beach for families.

Lahaina/West Maui

Lahaina Beach

Amenities: Swimming and Snorkeling.

Location:

Off of Front St., just North of Lahaina Shores Beach Resort.

Just North of the Lahaina Shores Beach Resort, this is a great beach for swimming and snorkeling. Also a favorite spot for canoe launching. Just off the road and a short walk to the shops off front street. A nice spot to get a little sun and cool off.

Lahaina/West

Puamana Beach

Location:

Off of Honoapiilani Highway near mile marker 19. Just South of downtown Lahaina.

Amenities: Restrooms, picnic areas, swimming and showers.

A very busy beach, crowded on weekends and holidays. The waves are usually good for beginner and intermediate surfers.

Lahaina/West Maui

Launiupoko Beach

Location:

Off of Honoapiilani Hwy, across from Kai Hele Ku St. Between Mile marker 18-19.

Amenities: Restrooms, picnic area, swimming and showers.

Green Grassy park with picnic tables and BBQ, Great for surfing and paddle boarding. Also has a lava rock wall pool area, great for kids.

Lahaina/West

189

Oluawala Beach

Location:

Located off of Honoapiilani Hwy, at mile marker 14 heading towards Lahaina.

Amenities: Snorkeling, swimming and surfing.

Long narrow beach, a popular local spot for surfing and a shallow coast great for snorkeling. The waters are loaded with beautiful coral, but please don't step on the coral. Be aware of the shark sighting posts, they are there for a reason.

Lahaina/West

Ukumehame Beach

Location:

Off of Honoapiilani Hwy at mile marker 12.

Amenities: Restrooms, picnic areas, swimming and snorkeling.

Great fishing and surfing beach. Just past the tunnel from Ma'alaea to Lahaina. At the West end of this reef creates the Thousand Peaks. Making this a popular beach for beginning surfers.

Lahaina/West

Papalaua Beach

Location:

Off of Honoapiilani Hwy located between mile marker 11-12.

Amenities: Restrooms, picnic areas, swimming and snorkeling.

Also called Thousand Peaks Beach. Bodyboarders and long boarders love this long sandy beach. At the East end is a spot called Coral Gardens, a great snorkeling spot.

Lahaina/West

Kapoli Beach

Amenities: None

Off of Honoapiilani Hwy 30 by Maalaea Harbor. Located at the northern most part of the harbor.

Local beach, some swimming and fishing areas. This beach is very small and tucked away. Probably not one for many to visit but pretty in its own way.

Maalaea/South

Sugar Beach

Amenities: Swimming and snorkeling.

Location:

Off of South Kihei Rd and Hwy 310.

Around three miles long goes all the way to Ma'alaea. One of the longest white sand beaches in the world. Some of the best sunsets can be seen from this beach.

Kihei/South Maui

Mai Poina Beach

Location:

Off of South Kihei Rd, South of Ohukai Rd.

Amenities: Restrooms, picnic areas, swimming, snorkeling and showers.

This beach borders with Sugar Beach and stretches about a mile from end to end. Great area for windsurfers.

Kihei/South Maui

Kalama Beach Park

Off of South Kihei Road. Main entrance to the beach is off of South Kihei Rd and Keala Pl.

Amenities: Restrooms, picnic area, swimming and snorkeling.

Not much sandy beach area, but plenty of room for large families and parties. Basketball, baseball, soccer and tennis also well lit volleyball courts. There is also a small skate park and roller rink for hockey. Great spot for surf lessons and standup paddle boarding.

Kihei/South

Cove Park Beach

Amenities: Showers

Off of South Kihei Rd, about half way in the middle of Kihei.

Small little beach perfect for beginners wanting to try their hand at surfing. Calm and shallow water great of kids.

Kihei/South Maui

Charley Young Beach

Location:

On the North end of Kama'ole I Beach off of South Kihei Road.

Amenities: Showers, swimming and snorkeling.

Great views, terrific sand and most think of it as one of the best beaches in Kihei. Just South of Kalama Park there is a small road that leads to this pretty beach across from Maui Vista Resort.

Kihei/South Maui

206

Kama'ole I

Location:

Off of South
Kihei Road/
Alanui Ke'ali'i
St.

Amenities: Restrooms,
picnic area, swimming,
snorkeling, showers and

The largest of the three
Kam's, great swimming
beach. One of the most
popular in the Kihei area.

Kihei/South Maui

Kama'ole II

Location:

Off of South Kihei Road/ Across the Street from Moose McGillycuddy's Restaurant

Amenities: Restrooms, picnic area, swimming, snorkeling, showers and lifeguards.

The smallest of the three Kam's, great swimming beach. One of the most popular for body surfing and boogie boarding.

Kihei/South Maui

Kama'ole III

Off of South Kihei Road. Just past Keonekai Rd.

Amenities: Restrooms, picnic area, swimming, snorkeling, showers and lifeguards.

A great swimming beach. One of the most popular for the locals, has a large grassy area for family gatherings and always packed on the weekends.

Kihei/South

Keawakapu Beach

Location:

Off of South Kihei road, take this road to the very end and stay right.

Amenities: Restrooms, swimming, snorkeling and showers.

According to some, this is the best beach for portrait photography. A very long and beautiful beach in front of a private residence.

Wailea/South

Mokapu Beach

Location:

Off of Wailea Alanui Dr and Ulua Beach Road. Just North of the parking area.

Amenities: Restrooms, swimming, snorkeling and showers.

Great beach for sunbathing and beginner divers. Snorkeling is great also when the waves are calm.

Wailea/South

Ulua Beach

Location:

Off of Wailea Alanui Dr. By the Grand Wailea and Four Season Resorts.

Amenities: Restrooms, swimming, snorkeling and

Great beach for dawn and dusk beach walkers and joggers. This is a great 1/4 mile long sandy beach, and usually more crowded than the beaches that are on either side. A good family beach and beautiful scenery out on the ocean and the Wailea Resorts.

Wailea/South

Wailea Beach

Location:

Off of Wailea Alunui Dr, between The Grand Wailea and Four Seasons Resorts.

Amenities: Restrooms, picnic areas, swimming and

Long, narrow and shallow beach. Great for fisherman and many locals use this beach. There is a paved walk way that runs behind the beaches of Wailea, that allows you a beautiful walk, stroll or jog anytime of the day.

Wailea/South

Polo Beach

Location:

Off of Wailea Alanui Dr., turn South bound on Kaukahi St.

Amenities: Restrooms, picnic areas, swimming, snorkeling and showers.

This is a beautiful beach, often crowded because of being by the resorts but beautiful scenery makes this a favorite.

Wailea/South

White Rock Beach

Amenities: Swimming and snorkeling.

Off of Wailea Alanui Dr and Kaukahi Street. Veer to the left onto Makena Rd.

Also known as Palauea Beach. Beautiful sandy beach, great snorkeling to the left or right of the beach. Not many tourists, some shade.

Makena/South

Secrets Beach

Amenities: Swimming

Location:

Off of Wailea Alanui Dr, right on Makena Rd, then SB just after the Wailea Golf Club.

Turn right into the parking lot. After you park, facing the ocean take the trail to the right and follow down to the beach. The trail is a little rocky but easy to follow. This is a great swimming beach, not rocky has a sandy bottom and a crescent shape. On the far North end of this beach some like to bath nude. Again this is not legal on the island but it does happen. This is also a great spot to see turtles as they frequent this beach.

Makena/South

Po'Olenalena Beach

Location:

Off of Wailea Alanui Dr., right on Makena Rd., South Bound just after the Wailea Golf Club.

Amenities: Restrooms, swimming and snorkeling.

Secluded white sandy beach, usually less crowded than its sister beach Makena Big Beach. Popular beach for weddings and great snorkeling at both ends of the beach.

Makena/South

Makena Landing

Location:

South from Wailea on Wailea Alanui Dr, continue on Makena Rd, turn right to stay on Makena Rd to Makena Landing.

Amenities: Restrooms, swimming and snorkeling.

Underwater sea caves and reef sharks. Great for snorkeling and divers. Great Kayake Launching area and very calm waters.

Makena/South

Malu'aka Beach

Location:

Located next to the Maui Prince Hotel. Turn off just before the Maui Fish Taco Stand.

Amenities: Restrooms, picnic areas, swimming,

Some think of this beach as the best swimming in Makena. Swimmers be aware of submerged boulders not visible in high tide.

Makena/South

Black Sand Beach

Location:

Off of Makena Alanui Road there is a dirt access road just South of the Grand Wailea Resort just before Big Beach.

Amenities: Swimming and Snorkeling

Also known as Naupaka Beach, unlike other black sand beaches that are made up of ground coral and shells, this beach is made up of ground lava. Snorkeling, sea life and coral are crazy here. Beautiful underwater scenery for snorkeling and divers.

Makena/South

Little Beach

Location:

Off of Wailea Alanui Dr/ Makena Alanui Rd Southbound, park at Big Beach and walk South over hill.

Amenities: Swimming and snorkeling.

Also known as Pu'u Ola'i Beach. Located at the end of Big Beach just over the hill. Also called naked beach as this is a favorite spot to take it all off.

Makena/South

Big Beach

Location:

Off of Makena Alanui Road. After Big Beach but before La Perouse Bay.

Amenities: Restrooms, picnic area, swimming.

Also known as Oneloa Beach. About 1 mile long, there are three entrances and parking areas for this beach. The first two entrances are the best with the third being a parking only and then there is a walk through the trees to get to the beach. Large swells, not recommended for small children to swim and not good for snorkeling. This is the longest, undeveloped white sand beach.

Makena/South

Secret Secret Beach

Location:

Off of Makena Road, Entrance is between two lava walls.

Amenities: None

Also known as Paako Cove. Parking is limited and the beach hard to find. Driving towards Makena Beach it is the third entrance by the lava wall. This is a great little secluded crescent shaped beach.

Makena/South

Hamoa Beach

Location:

Just past Hana, off of Haneo'o Road.

Amenities: Restrooms, swimming, snorkeling and

One of "Maui's Best Beaches" year after year, and one of Hana's most famous beaches. Surrounded by beautiful cliffs on both sides with green lush vegetation all around.

Hana/East Maui

Koki Beach

Location:

Off of Hana
Hwy mile
marker 49 & 50,
Southbound and
Haneo'o Road.

Amenities: Picnic areas and
swimming.

A beautiful red cliff beach.
You can swim here but read
the signs that are posted first.
More of a great place to
sunbath and picnic.

Hana/East Maui

Red Sand Beach

Location:

Take Ua'kea road past Hana Bay to where it dead ends. You then walk thru the field to start the trail.

Amenities: Swimming and snorkeling.

Also known as Kaihalulu Beach. DO NOT Swim past the lava sea wall, the strong currents are deceiving. A hard to find beach and a steep climb down. Beautiful but most choose not to adventure because of the risks and rocky conditions.

Hana/East

Hana Beach Park

Location:

Located right in the heart of Hana. Off of Hana Hwy on Keawa Pl, follow to the Beach Park.

Amenities: Restrooms, picnic area, swimming, snorkeling, showers and life guards.

Lifeguards are available for summer months only. Great for watching outrigger canoe races. This beach is approximately 700ft long and 100ft wide and is one of the safest swimming beach for kids.

Hana/East

Black Sand Beach

Location:

Hana Hwy, mile marker 32 at Wai'anapanapa State Park.

Amenities: Restrooms, picnic area, showers, good swimming.

Best Black Sand Beach on the island. Beautiful scenery and sea caves, and great coastal walks. Also called Papilla Beach.

Hana/East

Ho'okipa Beach Park

Amenities: Restrooms, picnic area, showers and lifeguards

Location:

Along Hana Hwy towards Haiku, around mile marker 9.

Windsurfing Beach, known for its world class surfers. Not a swimming beach and should be used by the experienced surfers and kite surfers. A great way to spend the day, have a picnic and enjoy the talent.

Paia/North Shore

Mama's Fish House

Amenities: None

Location:

Next to the restaurant Mama's Fish House.

Small sandy beach, shallow and great for kids. Also known as Kuau Cove. Parking is limited as it is tucked behind the restaurant, so there are just a few spots available. This is also a great beach to take a nightly stroll after dinner before heading back to your hotel.

Paia/North Shore

Tavares Bay Beach

Amenities: None

Location:

Location:

1/2 mile past the Paia traffic light. Look for the ceramic blue tile roof house, if you blink you will miss this beach.

Great for short boarders and body boards. Also known as Lamalani or Blue Tile House Beach.

Paia/North Shore

Paia Bay Beach

Location:

Off of Hana Hwy 36 at mile marker 6.2, just past Baldwin Beach, before you reach Baldwin ave.

Amenities: Restrooms and showers. Offers a skate park, basketball courts and also a youth center.

Great beach for boogie boarding and body surfing. The surf can get a little large so use caution when enjoying this beach.

Paia/North

Secret Beach (Paia)

Location:

Off of Hana Hwy 36, at mile marker 6.2, located between Paia Bay and Baldwin Cove.

Amenities: None

Clothing optional beach, very few visitors but very beautiful sand and the scenery is gorgeous. Just remember public nudity is illegal.

Paia/North Shore

H.A. Baldwin Beach

Amenities: Restrooms, picnic area, showers, good swimming and lifeguard.

Located off of Hana Hwy right before Paia on the left hand side.

This is one of the most popular beach park on Maui, as it is a great spot for boogie boarding because of the shore break. The beach is about 1 1/2 miles long and is made up of some beautiful white sand.

Paia/ North

Spreckelsville Beach

Location:

Hana Hwy 36 to Nonohe Rd and turn left. Then left on Paani Rd. Follow that road to the end and the ocean.

Amenities: Swimming and snorkeling.

Also known as Stables Beach. Just East of the airport. Two mile stretch, very windy on the beach side and on the rock side, it is a great fishing spot.

Spreckelsville/North

Kanaha Beach

Location:

Walking distance from Kahului Airport and accessible from Hana Hwy 36.

Amenities: Restrooms, picnic area, swimming, showers and lifeguards.

This beach offers a lot of possibilities. Kite boarding, wind surfing, swimming and fishing. Has a great place for a picnic.

Kahului/North

Kahului Beach Harbor

Location:

Piilani Hwy to E Kaahumanu Ave. It will be off of Hubron Ave.

Amenities: Restrooms, picnic area, swimming, snorkeling, outrigger canoe and paddlers.

Of all the things that this beach has to offer the locals love this beach as a great surf spot.

Kahului/North

Kite Beach

Location:

Located behind the Kahului Airport, Western end of Kanaha Beach.

Amenities: Swimming and lifeguards.

Known for being the best kite surfing beach. Located behind the airport. A great place to watch the professional kite surfers at work. This beach is also known as Ka'a Point and is divided into two areas "Old Hale Beach" (Old Man's Beach) and to the West Naisha Beach.

Kahului/North

Waihee Beach Park

Location:

Off of Hwy 340
and Halewaiu
Rd.

Amenities: Restrooms,
picnic areas, swimming,
snorkeling and showers.

This is a long and shallow
beach, great for fishing and
visited by many locals.

Wailuku/North Shore